LIFE ON A
VIKING
SHIP

JANE SHUTER

Heinemann Library
Chicago, Illinois

© 2005 Heinemann Library,
a division of Read Elsevier Inc.
Chicago, Illinois

Customer Service 888-454-2279
Visit our website at www.heinemann classroom.com

Originated by Modern Age
Printed in China by WKT Company Limited

09 08 07 06 05
10 9 8 7 6 5 4 3 2 1

Library of Congress Cataloging-in-Publication Data

Shuter, Jane.
  Life on a Viking ship / Jane Shuter.-- 1st ed.
      p. cm. -- (Picture the past)
  Includes bibliographical references and index.
  ISBN 1-4034-6441-3 (hc) -- ISBN 1-4034-6448-0 (pb)
  1. Vikings--Juvenile literature. 2. Viking ships--Juvenile literature.
I. Title. II. Series.
  DL65.S52 2004
  623.82'1--dc22
                              2004025848

Acknowledgments:
The publishers would like to thank the following for permission to reproduce photographs: AAAC p. **26**; AKG pp. **16**, **20** (Jurgen Sorges); Bridgeman p. **12**; Corbis pp. **9** (Ted Spiegal), **15** (Ted Spiegal), **22**; National Museum of Denmark p. **11**; Werner Forman pp. **7**, **8**, **10**, **18**, **19**; York Archaeological Trust pp. **6**, **14**, **24**, **27**.

Cover photograph of a stone carving of a Viking ship reproduced with permission of AKG.

Every effort has been made to contact copyright holders of any material reproduced in this book. Any omissions will be rectified in subsequent printings if notice is given to the publishers.

The paper used to print this book comes from sustainable resources.

Any words appearing in bold, **like this**, are explained in the Glossary.

Contents

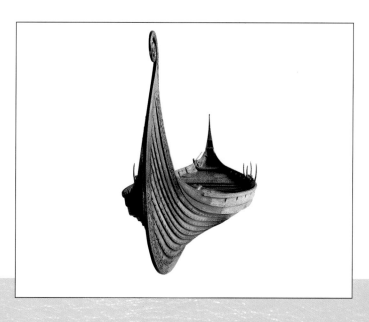

Who Were the Vikings?

The Vikings lived in Norway, Sweden, and Denmark more than 1,000 years ago. There were lots of different groups of Vikings, all with their own leaders. Ships were important to the Vikings for exploring, **trading**, and fighting. Without their shipbuilding and sailing skills, they could not have spread as widely as they did. They built all their ships in the same way, but used different shapes depending on what the ships were for.

Look for these: The longship shows you the subject of each chapter. The picture of a helmet shows you boxes with interesting facts, figures, and quotes about life on a Viking ship.

TIMELINE OF EVENTS IN THIS BOOK

A.D. 700 Vikings spread across Norway, Denmark, and Sweden

A.D. 780 First Viking raids on England

A.D. 795 First Viking raids on Ireland

A.D. 799 First Viking raids on France

VIKINGS MOVE ACROSS EUROPE, SAILING UP MAJOR RIVERS A.D. 800–850

A.D. 800

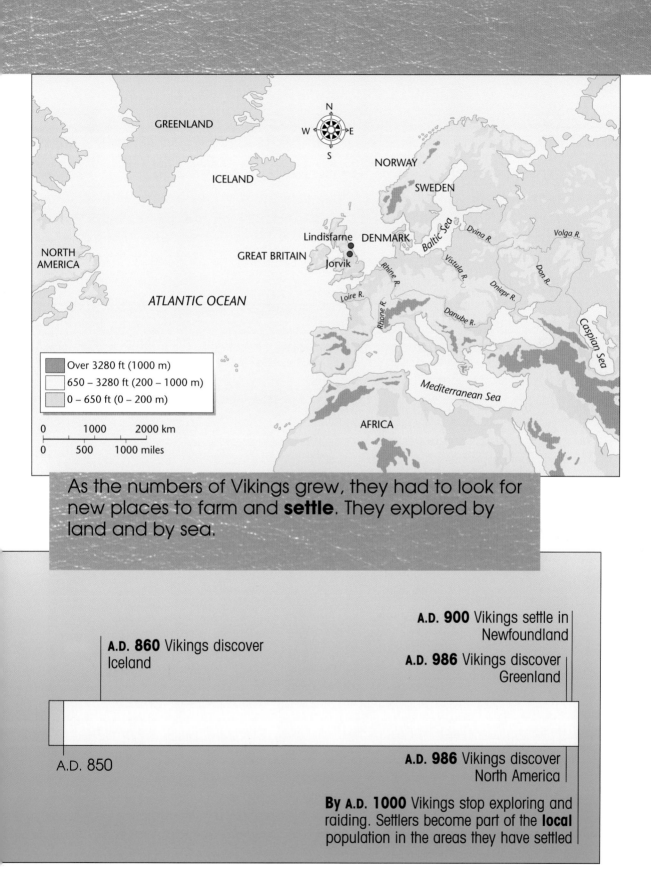

As the numbers of Vikings grew, they had to look for new places to farm and **settle**. They explored by land and by sea.

A.D. 900 Vikings settle in Newfoundland

A.D. 986 Vikings discover Greenland

A.D. 860 Vikings discover Iceland

A.D. 850

A.D. 986 Vikings discover North America

By A.D. 1000 Vikings stop exploring and raiding. Settlers become part of the **local** population in the areas they have settled

Viking shipmakers made their ships by hand. First they shaped the **keel** —the long piece of wood that ran along the center of the ship's bottom. Then they added the **end posts** that came up from the keel. They used overlapping planks to make the outside frame. Then they filled the gaps between the planks with a sticky, waterproof paste called **pitch**.

WOOD

The keel and the end posts of Viking ships were always made from oak. This is because oak is a strong wood. They used oak for the rest of the ship if they had enough. If not, they used other woods such as ash, elm or pine.

Viking shipbuilders used simple tools, like these. They split wood planks apart by banging wooden wedges into them with the ends of their axes.

Once the outside was finished, the shipbuilders made the inside **ribs** that ran across the ship to strengthen it. Then they made a block of wood to hold the **mast**. Boards were put across the ribs to make it easier to move around. The boards were lifted to **bail** water out of the ship. This was done often in bad weather, because the ships had low sides.

This is a copy of the Viking Gokstad ship, discovered in 1880, in Norway. It was a *karfi*—a king's ship that could be used for travel or fighting. It had been used in the burial of a Viking king.

Sailing Equipment

Once the basic shape of the ship was made, Viking shipbuilders had to add a **mast**, sails, and a **rudder** to steer the ship. The mast attached to a big wooden block in the middle of the ship and held up the single sail. The sail was big and almost square. It was moved up and down using ropes and weights. The rudder was like a big **oar** attached to the back of the right side of the ship.

Viking ships had **anchors**, like this one, made from iron or wood. The anchor held the ship steady in port or during a fight at sea.

The ship also needed oars, to use when there was no wind, or when the sail was taken down during fighting. Viking sailors also brought supplies for repairing the ship: spare cloth, thread, rope, and tools. These were stored in the chests that the Vikings sat on to row the ship.

This carving shows a Viking ship with its sail up. The lines across the sail may have been strips of leather or rope, used to keep the sail's shape.

The Vikings used their sails as often as possible. If they had to sail in the direction the wind was coming from, the sail did not work, so they rowed the ship. If they did not have enough people to row, they would then sail in a zigzag path. This way they used the wind one way, then the other. But it took a long time.

The Vikings used weathervanes like this brass one to work out which direction the wind was blowing.

The Vikings used to **navigate** by keeping close to the coast and remembering **landmarks**. If they were out of sight of land, they had to rely on the sun or the stars. They invented the pelorus, which was a compass that let them navigate using the shadows made by the sun. But when the weather was cloudy for a long time, they could get lost.

SAILING WEATHER

The Vikings rarely sailed at sea during the winter. A Viking book of advice on sailing, written in 1230, said:
"Only set out at the best time. Always have good equipment on your ship. Never stay out at sea too late in the autumn if you can avoid it."

This is part of a pelorus, or Viking compass. The whole thing would have been in the shape of a circle.

Warships

Viking **warships** were long and narrow. They floated very well on the water. Their **masts** could be taken down. All this was so they could sail up rivers, as well as at sea. The Vikings were well known for making surprise attacks on towns and villages by sailing up rivers that bigger boats could not use.

Some warships had carved animal heads like this that were put into the **end posts** of the ship to frighten the enemy.

The Vikings measured warships by how many **oars** the ship had. An average size was 28 oars which needed at least 28 rowers on board. A ship like this was about 55 feet (17 meters) long and 8 feet (2.5 meters) wide. The biggest warship that we know about had 60 oars and the smallest had 24.

The Viking shields fixed onto a piece of wood that ran along the side of the ship. When the Vikings landed, they just lifted them off.

Viking Battles

The Vikings did not like to fight out at sea. They liked to fight close to land, in calm water. Before a battle, they put their ships' **masts** down and tied several ships together. This made them less likely to roll over during the fighting. The biggest ship, the king's ship, was in the middle. Some ships were left free, to sail behind the enemy's ships.

The Vikings usually wore very plain, thick helmets. They were shaped to protect a man's face and neck in battle.

The battle began with the warriors firing arrows and throwing stones and spears at the enemy ships. They wanted to cause as much damage as they could before getting close. Once the enemy ships were close enough, the Vikings boarded them and fought hand-to-hand, with swords, spears, and axes.

This carving, found on the Island of Lindisfarne, is believed to show Viking warriors with swords and axes.

THE LOSERS

A Viking poet, writing about his king's victory, described the enemy in this way: "Those who were hurt threw themselves under benches, left their behinds sticking out, rammed their heads on the **keel**. Their warriors, when pelted with stones, turned their swords round to ride on their backs and fled."

Trading Ships

Trading ships were designed to carry **cargo**. The hold, used for storing **goods**, was 6.5 feet (2 meters) deep. Warships had a hold about 3.2 feet (1 meter) deep. Most trading ships were sailed by five or six people. Often these people were sharing the boat. They bought the boat and the goods together, sailed and traded, then split up the money they made.

HOW BIG?

Trading ships came in many sizes, but were smaller than warships. An average size was 50 feet (15 meters) long and15 feet (4.5 meters) wide. It would have had about 12 **oars**, although they were rarely used. A ship this size could carry about 20 tons of cargo.

This trading ship was found by underwater **archaeologists**. They put it back together and repaired it, so we can see what it looked like long ago.

Trading ships often towed smaller boats with them. These could take things further upriver.

Jorvik, now called York, in England, was a busy Viking port. It was not on the coast, but up the Ouse River. The river was deep enough for the Viking ships to sail up to Jorvik easily.

Trade

We know that the Vikings used to **trade** widely, because **goods** from many parts of the world have been found in Viking graves. They traded through the Mediterranean Sea and up long, wide European rivers like the Volga.

A KING'S FEAST?

The Viking king who was buried in the Gokstad ship was buried with many possessions. These included horses, dogs, and a peacock, which must have come from around India. We do not know if the peacock was buried as an expensive pet or an expensive meal!

This statue of Buddha, from India, was found in a Swedish grave. It shows just how far Viking traders traveled.

The Vikings traded fur, fat, fish, and **slaves** for wine, silk, and spices. Traders often carried their own scales and weights, to make sure they were not cheated. They traded the goods they bought at trading towns around the Viking world.

These coins, found in Sweden, came from many places in the Viking world. They include Arabic coins. The Arabs traded widely too.

Explorers' Ships

The Vikings went exploring in ships that were more like **cargo** ships in shape, with deep holds, but which had more **oars**. It was the Viking men who went exploring. Sometimes, several ships went together, led by the king. They explored by working their way along from one island or piece of mainland to another.

GETTING READY

Ships had to carefully prepare to go into the open sea. A book from 1230 says, "You should paint your ship well with **pitch** in the autumn and let it dry all winter. Have a share in a good ship, or in no ship at all."

This is a modern copy of Viking homes at Vinland, along the coast of North America. The builders used the same tools as the Vikings did.

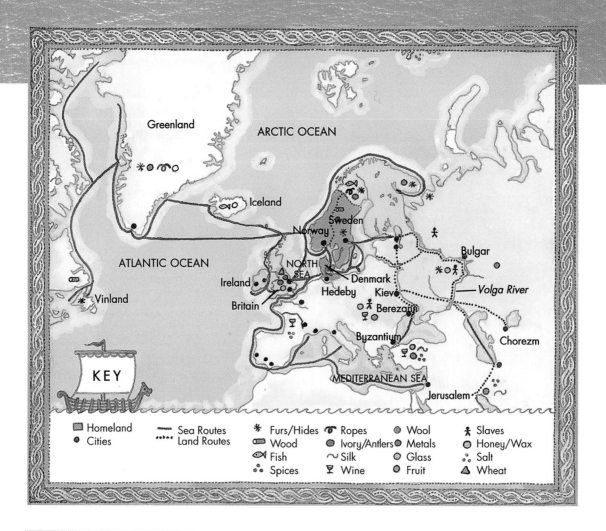

Greenland

ARCTIC OCEAN

Iceland

Sweden

Norway

ATLANTIC OCEAN

NORTH SEA

Denmark

Ireland

Hedeby

Kiev

Bulgar

Britain

Berezan

Volga River

Vinland

Byzantium

Chorezm

MEDITERRANEAN SEA

Jerusalem

KEY

⬛ Homeland	▬ Sea Routes	✳ Furs/Hides	☛ Ropes	◉ Wool	🚶 Slaves
◉ Cities	⬝⬝⬝ Land Routes	▭ Wood	◉ Ivory/Antlers	◉ Metals	◉ Honey/Wax
		⤳ Fish	∿ Silk	◎ Glass	∴ Salt
		∴ Spices	♉ Wine	◉ Fruit	△ Wheat

The Vikings explored to **trade** in new places, and often **settled** in places where they had started trading. This map shows how far the Vikings went.

The Vikings carried spare cloth with them, for mending the ship's sail. They also carried a wooden tent frame. They used the sail and the tent frame to make a covered area to eat and sleep in when they were not actually sailing. If they were close to land, they camped on the beach.

Exploration

The homeland of the Vikings, Denmark, Norway, and Sweden, did not have much good farmland. As the number of Vikings grew, they needed to explore to find new places to live. Explorers preferred to find land where there were few or no other people. But the Vikings fought for land if they had to.

FIRST SIGHTINGS

First descriptions of a new land almost always described how good it looked to **settle** on. So explorers said of Greenland, "the pasture is good, there are large, fine farms there." Explorers to North America said that there were plenty of salmon in the rivers and lakes, "bigger than they had ever seen."

The climate in the Viking homelands was cold. A great deal of land was too steep to farm on.

The Vikings found North America by accident. A merchant called Bjarni Herjolfsson sailed to Greenland in the year 985. He was blown off course and into fog. They finally found land, but it was too flat to be Greenland. Bjarni refused to go ashore and explore. He headed back for Greenland. As soon as he told what he had seen, others set off to find it.

When Vikings came to a place that was already lived in, they had to fight or make friends with the people living there. This was true even of other Viking groups.

Settlers' Ships

Settlers traveled in different ways, depending on how many of them were traveling and where they were going. Large groups set out on ships, like explorers. If just a few people wanted to settle in a place where Vikings already lived, they could travel on a **trading** ship going that way.

This Viking mold was used to make Christian crosses and tiny hammers, the symbol of the Viking god Thor. Some Viking settlers became Christian as part of settling in – others did not. So their blacksmiths made symbols for both religions.

The first thing Viking settlers did was build shelters for the animals they had brought and a shelter for their boat. Then they built houses for themselves. They lived in tents while they did this. Depending on the time of year, they began farming while the house was unfinished.

Viking settlers who came to a new place brought animals such as pigs and chickens with them.

Keeping Clean

Vikings homes had an outside toilet. They had a well that provided water for washing clothes and people. But how did the Vikings wash and go to the toilet while they were at sea? On short trips, they probably skipped baths altogether, especially in cold weather. On longer trips, or in hotter parts of the Viking world, they had to wash in seawater.

Buckets like this one were useful on board a ship for holding water to use for washing. People who did not want to hang over the side of the ship probably also used them as a portable toilet!

We do not know for certain about toilets, but it seems most likely that the Vikings used a bucket, or went directly over the side of the ship. The bucket was probably kept at the back of the ship. It could be emptied into the sea and cleaned with seawater every time it was used.

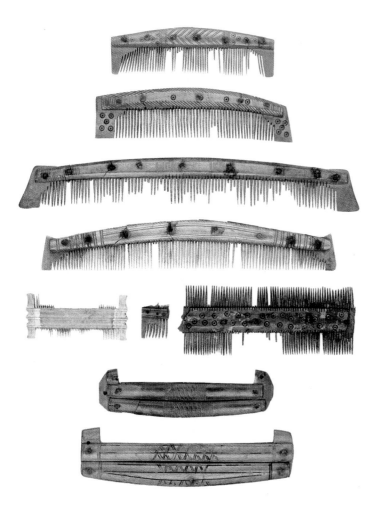

Viking women and some men and children had long hair. Most Viking men had beards. They kept their hair and beards clean and tidy by using very fine-toothed combs to get rid of any bugs or nits.

Food and Drink

The Vikings usually ate two meals a day. They had breakfast at sunrise and dinner in the evening when the sun set. They ate a lot of meat and even more fish, which they smoked, dried, salted, pickled, or ate fresh.

Vikings often had big feasts when they came home from sailing. The men ate, drank, and told stories. The women served the food and ate later, by themselves.

Flatbread

When they were sailing, the Vikings probably took little more than some flatbread and dried fish with them. If the bread got hard on long trips, they soaked it in seawater to soften it.

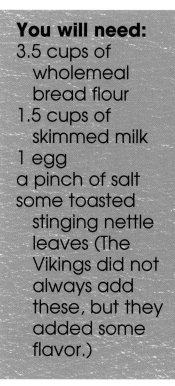

You will need:
- 3.5 cups of wholemeal bread flour
- 1.5 cups of skimmed milk
- 1 egg
- a pinch of salt
- some toasted stinging nettle leaves (The Vikings did not always add these, but they added some flavor.)

WARNING: Do not cook anything unless there is an adult to help you.

1 Heat the oven to 350°F (180°C).

2 Put the flour into a mixing bowl, make a hollow in the center of the pile and add the egg and half of the milk. Mix with your hands until all the milk has soaked into the flour.

3 Gradually add more of the milk, mixing with your hands as you go until it holds together in one big ball, but is not sticky (if it gets sticky, add more flour).

4 Knead the mixture, pressing and folding it over and over with your hands for at least 4 minutes.

5 Split the dough into pieces the size of a ping-pong ball. Press these pieces flat.

6 Bake in the oven, on a cookie sheet or on the oven rack, for about 10 minutes.

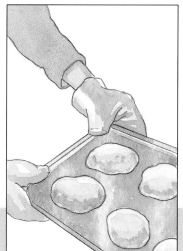

Glossary

anchor heavy object lowered from a ship to the bottom of the sea or river. It has ends that will dig into the bottom to hold the ship in one place.

archaeologist person who looks for objects from long ago to study how people lived in the past

bail to scoop water out of a ship

cargo things taken by sea to be traded

end posts pieces of wood at each end of the ship that come up from the bottom and hold the ship's sides in place

goods things that are bought, made, and sold

keel long, thick piece of wood that runs along the center of a ship's bottom

landmarks things on land which are easy to see, and used to navigate by. A landmark might be a funny shaped cliff, clump of trees, hill, or village.

local of a certain area

mast wooden pole that sails are hung on

navigate to work out how to get from one place to another

oars shaped pieces of wood used to pull ships through the water

pitch mixture made from the roots of a birch tree, used to make wooden ships waterproof

ribs pieces of wood that go across a ship to strengthen it, in the same way that our ribs go across our chests

rudder shaped piece of wood fixed to the end of a ship, which is used to steer

saga Viking adventure story

settle move from one place to live in another

slave person who is bought and sold by someone and has to work for that person

trade person's job; or the selling or swapping of goods

warship ship especially used for fighting

Further Reading

Books

Chapman, Gillian. *The Vikings*. Chicago: Heinemann Library, 2000.

Rees, Rosemary. *The Vikings*. Chicago: Heinemann Library, 2002.

Shuter, Jane. *The Vikings*. Chicago: Heinemann Library, 2003.

Index